Sheila The Sheep Goes To The Farm Show

Lively Livestock

By: Roxanne Dean

ISBN 13: 978-1530936502

ISBN- 10: 1530936500

Illustrations by

Sheila Gmeiner

DEDICATION

I dedicate this book to those who have shown their animals or entered any of the exhibits that are available at the Harrisburg Farm Show. There is always so much to do and so much to see. No one can get to see everything in one day.

Check Out The Animals Here!

**TIME FOR
THE SHEEP TO SHAWL CONTEST**

SO MUCH THAT WE TAKE FOR GRANTED
COMES FROM FARMS.! NOT ONLY FOOD
AND CLOTHING, BUT MANY OTHER
BY-PRODUCTS OF THINGS RAISED
ON FARMS !

CHAPTER ONE
PLANNING

Sheila couldn't wait to go to the

Farm Show.

Her main goal was to go the day

the "Sheep To Shawl Contest"

was held. One year her fleece

was used with another sheep that

combined two natural color

fleeces.

Thus the finished shawl received

the highest bid when it

was completed. Truly a work of

art! A local 4-H group in York

County competed as a group

at the Farm Show Arena for

the first time and managed to

sell their shawl at a top bid

that is still on the record books!

Natural colored wool means the

fleece was the color it was

sheared, right off the sheep.

It was not dyed but kept its own

distinctive color.

The group was happy to finish their

Shawl in the required time span,

let alone win a ribbon for fifth

place out of the eight teams

that were present that year!

Sheila sighed thinking about
how happy she was to take
part in such team spirit!
They were very happy at the
outcome.

A typical team consists of a
weaver, spinners, carders,
and a shearer.
Lots of equipment is setup ahead
of time. The loom has to be
started and a pattern designed

and modeled so that bystanders

can see what the finished

shawl would look like.

A sheep is brought into the

area and is sheared and the raw

fleece becomes carded so that

the wool is ready for the spinners

in long strips.

The strips are then spun into yarn

and ready for the weaver to

weave into a preset pattern.

There was a finished shawl on display so everyone could see what the teams would be working with. Then when the shawl at the Farm Show was completed it was put on a table so that the judges could examine it and give it points. Later that evening someone in the group would

model the shawl as it was

auctioned off to the highest

bidder.

Sheila wanted to get into that area

early enough after the shawls

were completed to see which one

would outbid all the others.

She read the pamphlet she had

picked up earlier.

"ThePennsylvania Farm Show Complex &
Expo Center is a large exhibition center
and indoor arena in Harrisburg,
Pennsylvania. It is primarily used for
concerts, agricultural exhibitions, the
Pennsylvania Farm Show, and indoor
football."

Pennsylvania is proud to host the largest
indoor agricultural exposition in the
nation, with nearly 6,000 animals,

10,000 competitive exhibits and 300 commercial exhibits.

Sheila thought back to the year
When her fleece was used to create
the shawl that was still on the record
books for the amount of money it
went at that auction.
When her owner brought it home to
 wash and block it and showed her
what it looked like, she was
extremely honored and happy!
Sheila's bubble burst when one of
the ewes in the herd called her
name. "Sheila!" "Sheila!" "Are you
 dreaming?"

Baaed Trinity one of the younger ewes. "Ewe have an expression on your face that sure looks happy!" Trinity added.

"Oh my, yes!" Sheila answered.

"I was thinking about the time my chocolate colored wool was used in a Sheep To Shawl Contest, The 4-Hers entered!" She sighed dreamily.

"That's why we will go to the Farm Show this Thursday, so we can watch this year's contest."

She baaed. "I was looking at the booklet to see what teams will be entering the contest this year."

Trinity nodded and looked around the pasture.

"Which sheep are going with ewe this year?" She asked.

Sheila turned to Trinity and replied, "Only six of us can go this year, Trinity."

"Are ewe one of the sheep that picked a winning number out of the hat?" Sheila asked. "It had to be number one through five in order for ewe to be able to go!

I am the sixth one, obviously."

"YES!" Trinity almost jumped straight up in the air.

"I got number two!" She bleated happily.

"The others who got the remaining numbers consist of Laggy, Mary, Kells and Shancy." She added.

"Cool!" Sheila bleated. " I just hope Laggy stays with his group this time." Sheila sighed.

"He has been known to get into unusual situations In the past. He likes to wander around on his own and ewe have to stick together when there are lots of people everywhere." Sheila shook her head and looked down the pasture at Lagavulin, a Shetland ram with a beautiful grayish- white fleece.

His fleece had won many ribbons at the York Fair over the years for its beautiful crimpy texture. Laggy, as he was called, was also very

photogenic and won
several awards for his funny
photographs.

He liked to move his tongue
around when he saw food,
animal crackers, and other
 treats!

Chapter Two
The Day Arrives

All the sheep that were going

to the Farm Show jumped into

the van that was taking them to

Harrisburg.

It was a cool, brisk morning,

but at least it wasn't snowing or

sleeting. The sun was partly

covered with clouds but it

was a clear day for traveling.

The animals were excited

and ready for a day of

adventure. They couldn't

wait to see all the animals that

would be taking part in the

Show this year.

Shancy who was in the back of

the van was listening

very carefully since this was

the first time she would be going

to the Farm Show. She was

now big enough to go along

and was lucky enough to

pick one of the top numbers.

Shancy looked a lot like her mom, Sheila, except she had a fluff of white on top of her head and a white tipped tail and two white socks.

Shancy

It was a very exciting ride to

the Harrisburg Farm Show for

the sheep. The group talked

about what they had heard

from the others that had been

there before.

Three of the six sheep had

never gone, so they were not

only excited but a bit nervous.

They were not going to stray

from their group since they

didn't want to get locked up

in a pen somewhere and not

make it home.

After an hour long ride, the

van pulled up in a building

for animals to be escorted into

the small arena area.

The Celtic Herd sheep

huddled together and were

 finally escorted into a

small area so that each of

them could get their

special admissions pass.

They had to display it around

their necks so it was visible

 at all times.

Chapter Three
The Tour Begins

Sheila gave the schedule to each

of the sheep in case any of them

got separated and she warned

them not to take off for any

reason! They would get in as

much as possible before the

Sheep To Shawl contest began

later in the afternoon.

There was a photo in the booklet

with the information on all

the current teams that would be in

the competition along with some

of the events that would

be scheduled for that day.

The sheep passed a variety of

cattle and other

sights as they strolled along.

"This is so cool," baaed Mary

whose eyes were almost popping

out of her sockets!

When they passed the fleeces
on display the ewes ewe-d
and awed!

"Look!"Shancy squeaked.
"There is a Shetland Fleece in
the display case! It almost looks
like my fleece," she added.

They were interrupted by a cow who was very upset that they
were walking around by themselves.

"Hey ewe guys! What do ewe think you are doing out there?"

The cow mooed very loudly
and udderly loud!!!

"EWES are not allowed to wonder
around here!" She mooed
and started screaming to
attract attention.

Sheila motioned to the herd to keep
moving quickly away from that cow.

One of the ewes stuck her tongue
 out at the cow!
They decided to stop at the feed
area and get a drink of water
 and see what treats they could find.

There were slices of apples
and some cracked corn on one
of the tables with a sign
overhead that said

"WELCOME VISITORS!"

HELP YOURSELF!"

Some other animals were resting and others were getting a snack.

After everyone was rested and had a full stomach (all four of them), they

continued on their tour. There was so much going on, it was hard to take it all in and not stop and just stare.

Sheila asked the herd to stop for a minute and listen to some suggestions. She thought about her home and her pasture and how peaceful it was compared to this event!

Scene at Celtic Herd

Each of the sheep had their picture on their admissions badge for easy identification.

Roxanne Dean

Sheila was the only solid chocolate color out of the group.

Finnola

Trinity

Mary

Shancy

LAGGY

Handsome Shetland Ram

Lagavulin

The tour continued and Sheila
and her group stopped at each
open spot to see what animals

SHEILA AND HER HERD
TOUR THE ARENAS

occupied each of the pens.

The pigs didn't show much action!

There was a ram inside a pen who
was smiling at them as they waved
and walked around the arena.
He seemed to be in a good mood
and was comfortably sitting on a
pile of hay. It was rare to see an

animal sitting up like that.

He acted like a celebrity.

"I wonder who he is," Sheila said

to her group. Laggy just

made a sound of displeasure.

"He thinks he is really cool,"

Laggy baaed.

Another cow gave them a strange

look.

The produce looked amazing!
They were tempted to stop and
taste some of it, but Sheila shook
 her head!

Some of the cows looked very
relaxed. One in particular was very
friendly and wished them a good
day. Another cow was getting
lots of attention from her owner
and was obviously enjoying
getting her head scratched.

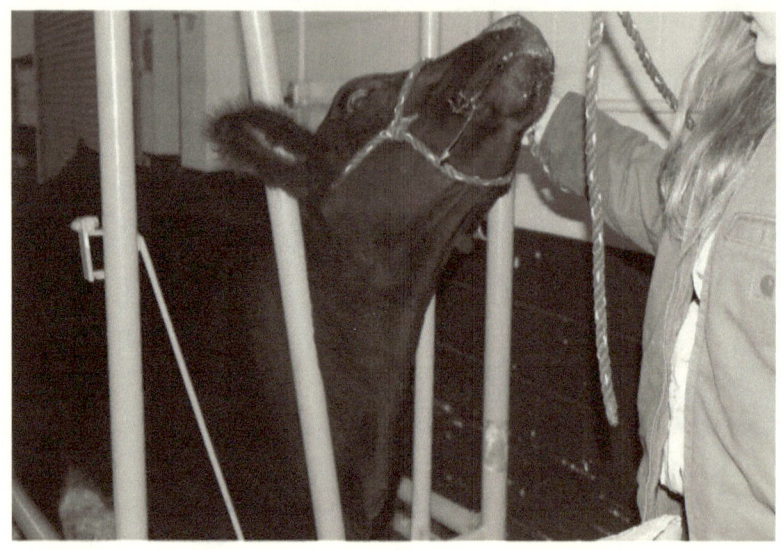

A Nice pet on the head feels good!

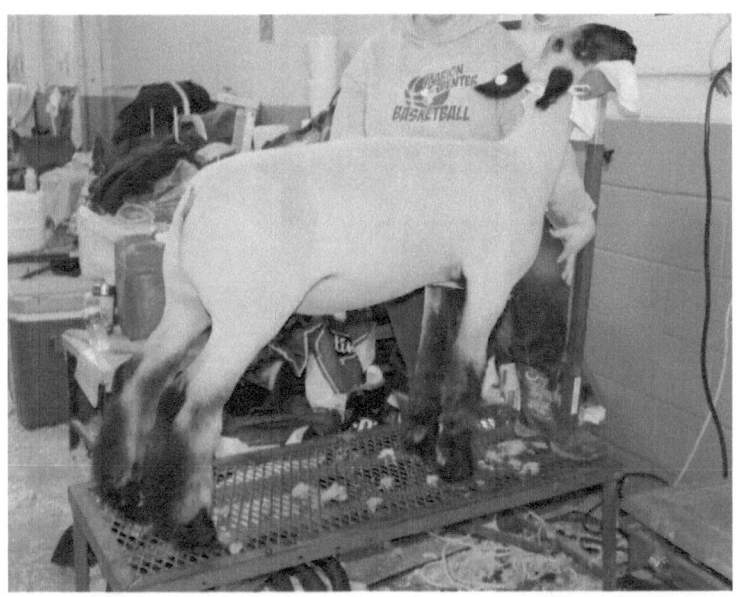

Getting Ready For The Show Ring

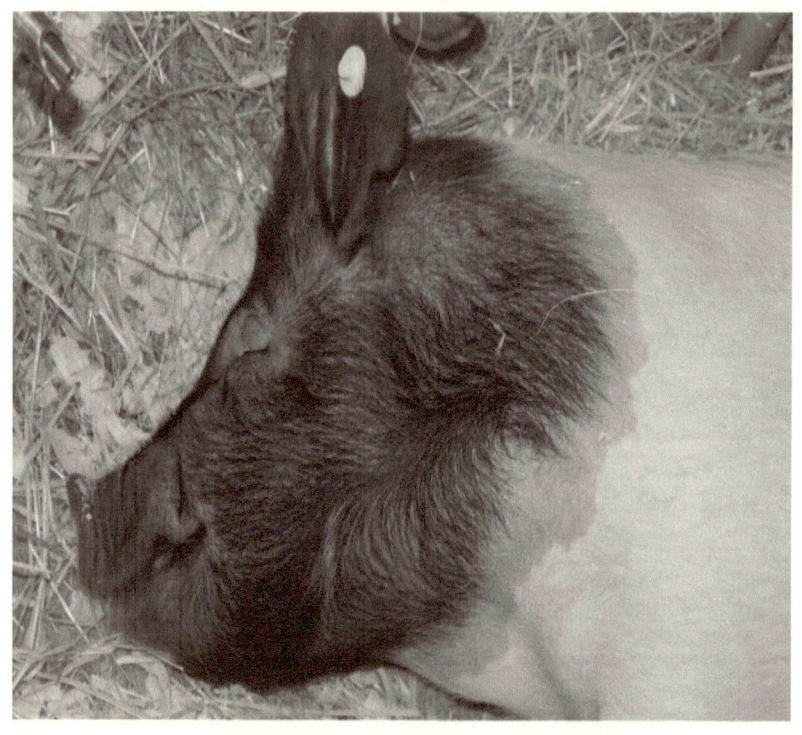

NAP TIME IN THE SWINE ARENA

Equine Activities

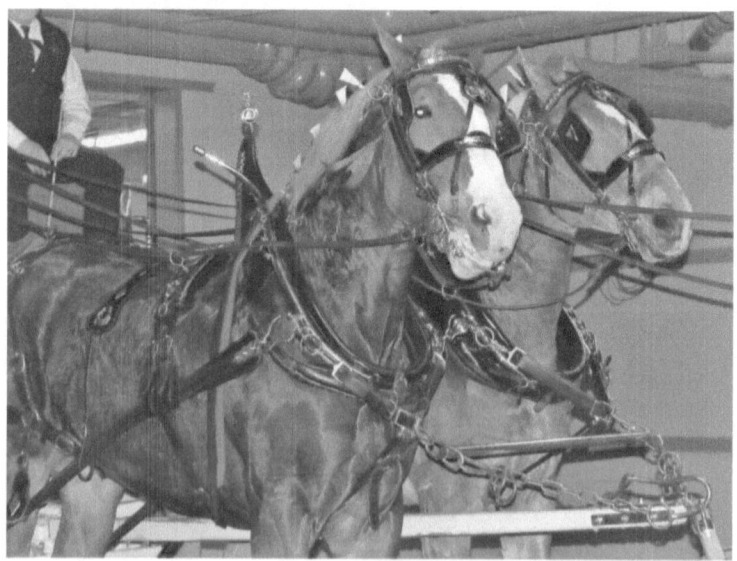

Market Lambs

Trinity was nervous when she
saw the market lambs and Sheila
told her they would be sold for
meat. "YIKES! That is scary
let's keep going."
Trinity screeched.

Bovine Discussion

The sheep were amazed at the

number of animals at the Farm

Show.

Laggy stopped to listen to a

conversation among two of the cows.

They turned and stared at him. They were obviously annoyed at his eavesdropping!

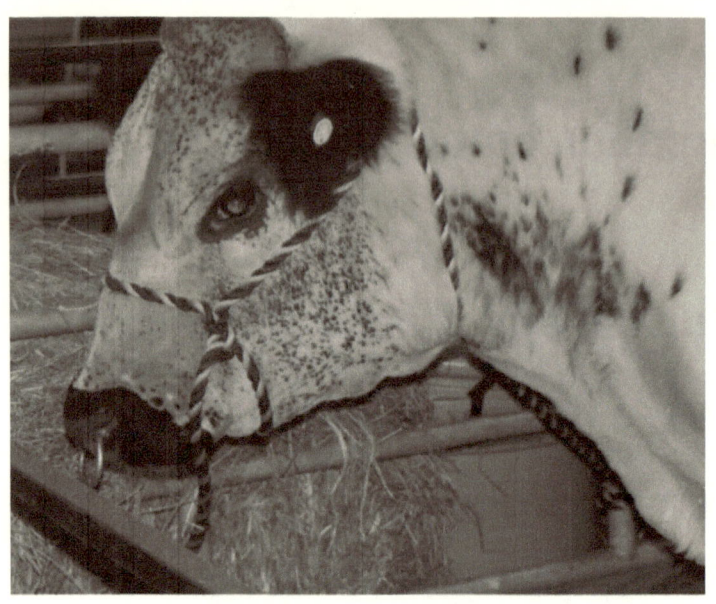

As they passed the carousel,

Laggy said he would like to ride

it and wondered If they could

 go on it.

The attendant who was working

 the carousel heard him and told

 him to go over to the next arena

and they could get a ride in a cart

 if they mentioned they were friends

of his so they said thanks and

walked over.

Chapter Four

Trouble

The herd went over to where they saw the carts and looked for someone who was in charge. Laggy stopped to look at some other animals.

He was amazed how they seemed
to be comfortable and not upset at
being kept in a pen.

He continued walking and was
soon out of sight of the rest of his
group.

Suddenly he was grabbed from
behind and a halter was wrapped
around his neck.

"Hey!" he started to yell but then
a bag was put over his head and
everything was dark.

Meanwhile, Sheila and the herd
managed to find the man in

charge of the carts and
were escorted to an empty
cart. They were excited
and ready for their ride around
the arena.

They rode around for almost an hour.

All of a sudden Sheila turned and looked in the back of the vehicle and realized that Laggy wasn't with them. "Where is Laggy?" Sheila shrieked. Shancy looked around and said, "We were so excited to ride in the cart, we didn't notice he wasn't here, oh no!"

"What are we going to do, Sheila?" Shancy asked. Sheila shook her head. "I think we better go to an information desk to have someone look for him," she said.

The herd quickly followed Sheila to look for an information desk and try to find Laggy.

Sheila looked at the clock and realized they needed to get to the Sheep to Shawl area in the next half hour. They walked quickly and headed in that direction, following the signs to the next building.

They came across an information booth and stopped to get help. Sheila told them what happened and the attendant made a call on

the intercom for assistance.

"We will be going to the Sheep
to Shawl contest,"
Sheila told the attendant.
"Please send him there if you find
him.
He should have his ID on him."
The group then filed out to find the
wool area where the Sheep to Shawl
contest would be held.
Shancy shook her head, "Laggy
seems to get in trouble without even
trying." she baaed.

They passed some other animals in various areas waiting to be shown in their individual contests.

There were swine, cow, farm displays, horses and then finally some sheep.

Finally they got through the crowds
and ended up in the right room.
"Wow, it takes a lot of coordinating
to get through these crowds. I am

glad you know where you're going

Sheila."Mary commented.

"This place is huge!" she added.

"There is so much going on here, I

hope we don't get separated like

 Laggy did.

Who Says This is For Birds?

"Well, I love the commotion and seeing all the animals." Shancy baaed. "As long as someone else knows where to go!"

CHAPTER FIVE
THE SHEEP TO SHAWL CONTEST

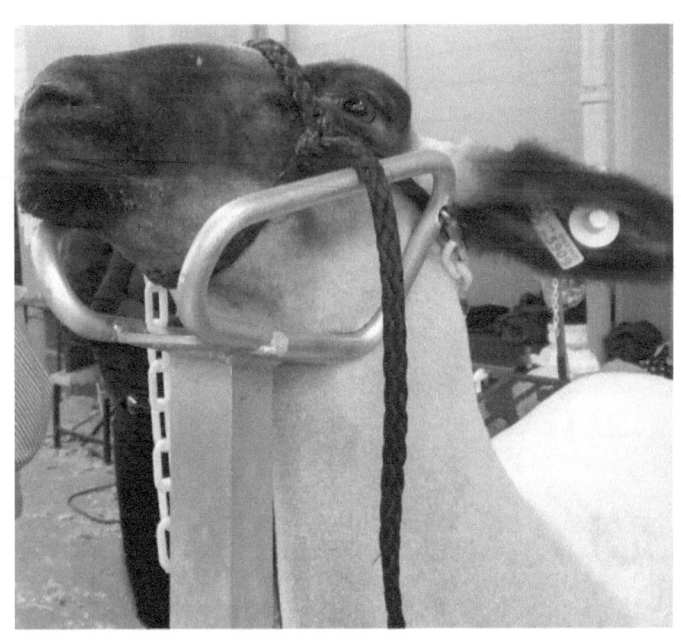

There were many contests going on including the Market lambs in the small arena but Sheila and her herd had their purpose in mind as they filed in to where the sheep to shawl contest was starting.

There were sheep in pens waiting to get sheared to be part of the shawls in progress.

The announcer would tell them when to begin and the excitement was obvious among the teams competing.

Each team had matching outfits and colors.

A sample of what the shawl would look like was on display next to each area where the teams would be working. There were looms, spinning wheels, and seats placed together so that the wool could be carded and then handed over to the spinners.

Then the spun wool would be handed over to the person in charge of the loom to be woven into the pattern they had preselected.

Visitors could walk around and see the shawls so they would know what to bid on when the auction started.

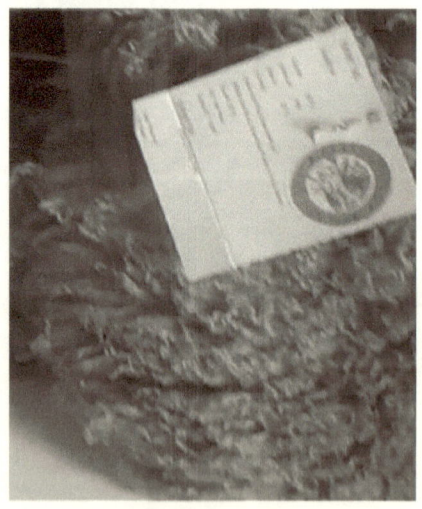

Shetland Fleece

All of a sudden, Sheila turned around

when she heard a familiar sound,

and lo and behold, there was Laggy

in one of the pens completely

sheared and looking embarrassed.

"What on earth happened ?"

Sheila shrieked and told the others to look Behind them. "Oh my goodness," Shancy yelled, "Laggy has been kidnapped and he is sheared. What are we going to do Sheila?"she asked very confused.

"Laggy doesn't have his ID anymore and he got put into one of the pens used for the contest."

Sheila told everyone. "His fleece must be used in one of the shawls and we are going to have to help him escape when everyone is preoccupied with the contest."

She added.

Work of Art -Sheep

"Okay girls, here is the plan." Sheila motioned for them to move closer and whispered how they we are going to get Laggy out. We will have to leave quickly as soon as he is out. So let's stay calm and watch some of the show so we don't have people looking at us suspiciously,"
she BAAED!

They watched the teams rush to get their shawls finished and run them up to the judges, where the shawls were spread out on a table. The winners were announced from first place to eighth place. An announcer told the crowd that the shawls would soon be modeled and ready for the auction.

As soon as everyone's attention was on the models up on the stage, Sheila gave a signal and two of the ewes walked past the pen where

Laggy was captured and bumped the latch.

Laggy immediately rushed out and the rest of the group pushed up behind him so it would be hard to separate him.

"Follow me!" Sheila whispered and the entire herd started running down the aisle into the open space where the hay was pulled.

Someone pointed to where they were hiding so they kept going .

They ran between the hay bales where there was an exit to the outside and kept going until they were safely outside.

Finally, they stopped to catch their

breath and looked around to see that everyone was safely out.

Laggy was shaking at this point and was gasping.

"Come on everyone, let's find our trailer!'

"We will just have to find out who won when we read it in the paper

or go on the Farm show website."

CHAPTER SIX

HOME SAFELY

Most of the ride home was quiet with an occasional snort or baa.

All of the sheep were still in shock about what had happened.

They couldn't believe they managed to get out in one piece literally that is- except for Laggy!

The ewes finally started talking about all the cool things they got to see and do, including the cart ride around the arena.

"I really liked that ram we saw." Mary sighed. "He was cute!" Shancy replied.

"It was definitely an interesting day, all the way around, even with Laggy getting penned." Sheila commented.

"Laggy ! what would you do without us!" She asked. She was starting to

get really hungry.

"I can't believe all the butter they use in the butter sculpture," Laggy finally chimed in, "I was so interested in looking at the displays, I didn't see those guys sneak up on me from behind."

"I bet you were scared when that happened!" Trinity added. " I would have been screaming my head off, how come you were so quiet?" she asked.

"Are you kidding?" Laggy replied, "There were people everywhere, I

was afraid they would knock me
over or something. As it turns out, I
got sheared and that shearer
was actually pretty good, it didn't
take him that long !"
The herd continued with their
highlights of the day until Trinity
announced she was extremely tired
and needed to call it a night.
The rest of the herd agreed it
was time to rest. Tomorrow
they would find out who won
the contest for the best shawl

and how much the shaw sold for.

"Goodnight everyone." Sheila said.

"We will chalk this up to just another

Adventure For "THE SHEEP OF

CELTIC HERD!

Tomorrow is another day ."

Sheila fell asleep dreaming about

the sights she had seen at The

Pennsylvania Farm Show.

Reptiles

Butter Sculptor

Working Horses

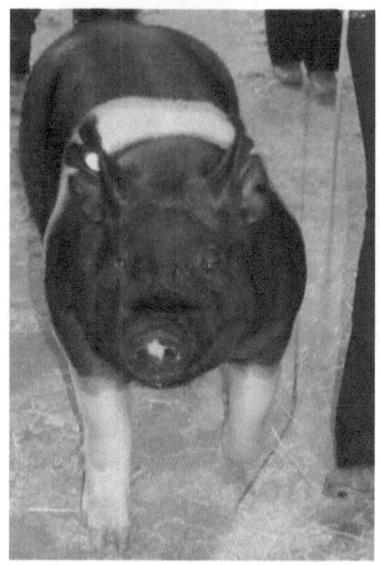

New Friends

Rodeo -Take a Photo

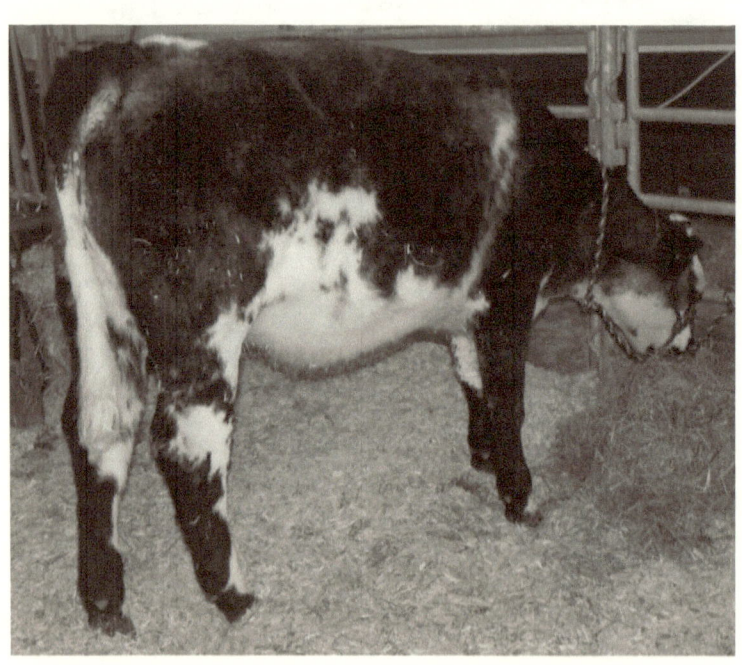

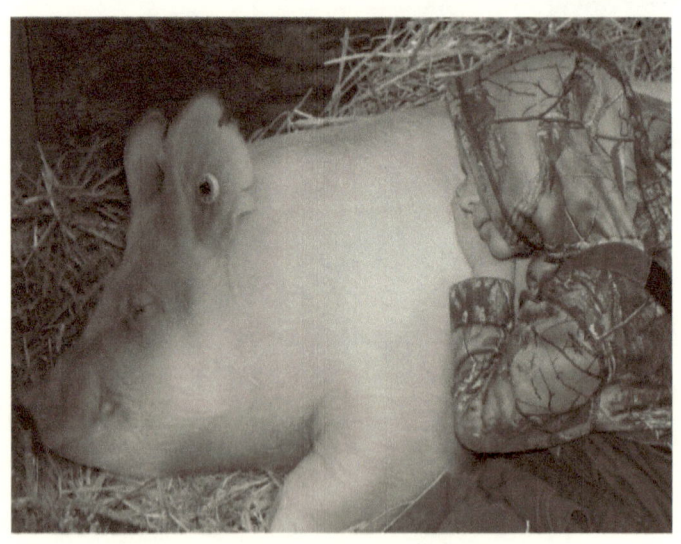

AWW KEEPING WATCH!

The next morning Sheila called the herd together and told them the news.

The headlines in the paper read:

Missing Ram -

Part of The Winning Shawl

The winning shawl at yesterday's "Sheep to Shawl" contest included the beautiful fleece of a Shetland Ram whose owner is not known at this time. Sometime during the contest, the ram escaped and was

not seen again.

If anyone knows the whereabouts of

this handsome creature, please

contact the Farmshow Office..........

Laggy just smiled and stuck out his tongue, It was snowing, after all it was Farmshow Week!!!!!!

THE END

Sheila Making Arrangements

For The Farm Show

Shetland Shawl and yarn from

" Laggy's" Fleece

Knitted by Rhianna Dean

Fun Trivia

There are over 1 billion sheep in the world, more in China than any other country.

Adult female sheep are known as ewes, while adult male sheep are known as rams, and their offspring are lambs. Between the ages of 1 and 2 a lamb is known as a hoggart, the significance is that once a lamb reaches the age of two, its meat becomes mutton.

In Wales a group of sheep is known as a flock (cail), but in other parts of the world the collective noun is herd or even a mob.

Interestingly, the plural of sheep is the same as the singular. Can you think of another mammal where this is true?

* Deer, bison, moose and possibly swine!

Sheep like to stay close to others, which makes them easier to move together to new pastures.

However, sometimes they are held in a sheepfold..

Sheep have a field of vision of around 300 degrees, allowing them to see behind themselves without having to turn their head.

Sheep are herbivores that eat vegetation especially grass.

The digestive system of sheep features four chambers which help break down what they eat.

If a sheep falls on its back, with all

four legs in the air, it's becomes

 stuck and cannot right itself without

help from a farmer.

In 1996, a sheep named Dolly was

the first mammal to be cloned from a

somatic cell.

Sheepfold

Celtic Herd

Winning Photo with Laggy-York Fair

Other books by Roxanne Dean

Harley is excited that he will be walking in the annual Alexandria Scottish Christmas Parade. This event takes place in Old Town Alexandria Virginia. It is a tradition to have Scottish Pipebands and Scottish dogs walk in this parade which is held the first Saturday of December. The event takes place regardless of the weather. Harley is going to walk with his Scottish Westie friends, Duffy and Jasper and can't wait. He knows the weather has gotten colder and soon it will be time for the parade. He can't wait to hear the tunes from the bagpipers. He also gets to tour an historical town, and see all the dogs dressed up in their Scottish and Christmas attire!

CAN'T
HARLEY WAIT!
ROXANNE DEAN

Barcode Area
We will add the barcode for you.
Made with Cover Creator

Alexandria Va.- Annual Christmas Scottish Walk

WHERE'S HARLEY?

Roxanne Dean

A PHOTO JOURNAL OF RAIL TRAILS IN SOUTHERN YORK CO.

Pennsylvania

Codorus State Park

Beach

Herding Dogs

Fun On Shearing Day

Point Of View of

Sheep

Roxanne Dean ∞ Sheila The Sheep Goes To The York Fair

FIRST PLACE

FAIR

Sheila The Sheep Adventures
A Day Out for Ewe!

York Fair

Scottish Music-Scottish Sheep

All books appropriate for all ages Elementary Level and adults. Fiction and Nonfiction.

Information included in all books.

Other information available

on Facebook page: RoxyDean Author.

Coming Spring:: **Sheila The Sheep Rides The New Freedom Steam Train**   **2018**

EWE ARE LOVELY!

Winning Shetland Shawl

Sheila 's Fleece